Original title:
Space Oddity Odes

Copyright © 2025 Creative Arts Management OÜ
All rights reserved.

Author: Ophelia Ravenscroft
ISBN HARDBACK: 978-1-80567-852-6
ISBN PAPERBACK: 978-1-80567-973-8

Echoing Dreams Across the Cosmos

In a tin can zooming high,
A cat with goggles says goodbye.
She floats and spins, a starry chase,
While sipping tea in endless space.

The moonlight winks, it knows the score,
As squirrels launch from a cosmic shore.
They dance on comets, twirl with glee,
In search of nuts for breakfast tea.

Asteroids whizz with a cheesy grin,
While aliens giggle at the din.
With silly hats and silver shoes,
They break the rules with crazy hues.

A cosmic choir sings off-key,
While shooting stars recite with glee.
They play charades in milky trails,
And send the universe their tales.

Radiance of the Falling Star

A comet sneezed, oh what a sight,
It sparkled glitter in the night.
Aliens laughed, they fell off chairs,
As cosmic confetti danced in pairs.

Planets wobbled, now that's bizarre,
When meteors get drunk at the bar.
Stars tried to twinkle through the haze,
But moon just giggled, lost in a daze.

A Time Capsule in the Milky Way

In the Milky Way, what a jam,
Space penguins play a cosmic game.
They send back selfies, please respond,
A meandering dance, so frolicsome and fond.

Asteroids roll like bowling balls,
While satellites have raucous brawls.
A time capsule full of jokes untold,
Laughs echo through space, manifold.

Nebula's Cry

A nebula sighed, 'Oh dear me!'
As stardust spilled from its leafy tree.
It coughed up colors, a radiant pop,
Whirls of laughter that never stop.

Galaxies giggled, with twinkling eyes,
Drawing funny faces in the skies.
The universe chuckles, a cosmic delight,
While planets spin, wrapped in the night.

Astral Ballet of the Cosmos

In an astral show, stars take the lead,
While black holes twirl at lightning speed.
Planets wear tutus, all in a line,
As comets leap high and brightly shine.

Dwarf planets bobbed, a quirky dance,
Galactic rhythms that put you in a trance.
The moon winks cheekily, joins in the fun,
A ballet of laughter, for everyone!

The Silence Between Worlds

In a vacuum where voices fade,
Yet stars dance like they're getting paid.
Aliens giggle, sipping their drinks,
While comets zip by, giving winks.

Gravity's pulling but I'm just a flake,
Floating along, it's a cosmic break.
Asteroids tumble, they can't find the groove,
We're all lost in this interstellar move.

Cosmic Ballet

Planets twirl in a grand pirouette,
Dancing with moons, no cause for fret.
Saturn's rings are quite the sight,
Flipping and flopping in the starlit night.

Stars are the audience, laughing aloud,
At meteor showers that draw a crowd.
A cosmic ballet with no rehearsals,
Just twinkling lights in universal swirls.

Lightyears of Longing

I wrote a letter to a star far away,
Tied it to a rocket, sent it today.
Lightyears of longing in this vast abode,
Hoping it travels down the cosmic road.

The mailbox is empty; it's getting old,
Did my words get lost in the void, uncontrolled?
Perhaps it's stuck in a black hole's embrace,
Or the star's on a vacation, enjoying its space.

Celestial Echoes

A loud boom echoes through the void,
Strange sounds of laughter—are we paranoid?
Asteroids chuckle, the Milky Way sighs,
As UFOs zoom by, offering pies.

Echoes of laughter ripple like waves,
In a universe where humor behaves.
Cosmic winds carrying jokes from afar,
In this strange theater, we are the stars.

The Universe's Lament

In the void, the stars do dance,
With cosmic shoes, they take a chance.
But every step, they trip and fall,
A clumsy waltz, they can't recall.

Galaxies spin like a wild tyke,
Their colors clash like bad bike hikes.
They mumble tunes of ancient lore,
While black holes snicker, wanting more.

Orbits of the Heart

Two planets whirl in playful guise,
With cheeky grins, they flirt and rise.
One rolls left, the other spins right,
In this game of love, it feels so light.

Asteroids chuckle, they can't resist,
"Make your move, or you'll be missed!"
While shooting stars and comets play,
Joking about their long delay.

Dreams in Quasar Light

In nebula beds, dreams grow wide,
Filled with laughter, they take a ride.
With quasar beams that tickle the night,
A cosmic giggle, pure delight.

Stars trade jokes with a meteor's wink,
"Did you hear about the black hole's stink?"
They snicker softly in the dark,
Creating sparks with every spark.

Darker than a Black Hole

In the shadows where silence lays,
A black hole grins in mysterious ways.
"It's darker here than a sock drawer,"
It chuckles softly, craving more.

Comets pass with a wink and a nod,
"Your jokes are bad, but hey, I applaud!"
In the universe's depths, laughter rings,
Even black holes can wear funny things.

Confessions from the Cosmos

In a rocket full of snacks,
Aliens stare with wide eyes.
Forget the stars and their flares,
I just hope my chips don't fly.

Floating through a cosmic jam,
I wave at Martians and cats,
They chuckle at my odd dance,
While I just sit and chat.

Asteroids roll like marbles,
As I try to take a sip,
But my juice is in zero-G,
And I'm wearing it like a drip.

Jokes from planets echo loud,
As I try to flip a switch.
A comet sideswipes my radio,
It's bleak, but also rich.

Fragments of Light

There's glitter in the void,
And a giggle in the beams.
Stars keep winking at me,
Like we share secret dreams.

I sent a postcard to the sun,
But it bounced right back to Mars.
Perhaps it's too far away,
Or it's busy with its stars.

Comets are just cosmic dogs,
Chasing tails through the night.
I wave and give a biscuit,
Each bounce a yelp of delight.

In the great expanse, I muse,
What's a planet's favorite dish?
Maybe it's stew or pizza,
Or something truly swish.

The Gravity of Dreams

I float on pillows of stardust,
Dreaming of sandwiches wide.
But no matter how I reach,
They float just out of my stride.

Gravity is such a prankster,
Pulling me down to the floor.
While dreams wave from the ceiling,
I leap and I try to soar.

I tripped on a meteorite,
Landed in a galactic pool.
Splashing with quirky aliens,
We laughed like it was a school.

One offered me cosmic fries,
With milkshakes from the stars.
I hesitated for a sec,
Then said, "Let's leave Earth behind!"

Moonlit Meditations

Underneath the crescent moon,
I ponder silly thoughts.
What if planets had hobbies,
Like knitting or tying knots?

The moon snickers from above,
While meteors race by fast.
I can't tell if they're happy,
Or just in a cosmic blast.

I wondered if stars get bored,
Twinkling in the sky at night.
Maybe they play hide and seek,
With comets zooming in flight.

In the glow of lunar whispers,
I giggle at the absurd.
Sometimes in the starlit quiet,
Joy is the best of words.

Wanderlust in Orion's Arms

In Orion's arms, I did a jig,
Floating high like a happy pig.
Stars are dancing, comets spin,
I lost my shoe, but found a grin.

Galaxies giggle as I glide,
With asteroid friends, I joyfully bide.
We sip on stardust, munch moon pies,
Who knew the universe could be so spry?

My rocket's got a sing-along,
With Martians chiming in with song.
Zero gravity's a clumsy dance,
I twirl and whirl, I miss my chance.

So lift your spirits, chase the beams,
In cosmic dreams, we'll sail on streams.
Laughter echoes through the night,
As I float on in pure delight.

Jupiter's Embrace

In Jupiter's arms, I found my place,
A giant hug in this vast space.
His storms whirl, a colorful twirl,
It's a wacky world, watch my hair curl!

With moons as buddies, we hop and skip,
Riding the winds on a cloudy trip.
We roast marshmallows on lightning's spark,
Singing songs till the night's grown dark.

Oh what a dance on this gas giant,
A bouncy party, oh so vibrant.
Floating high, I shout and cheer,
Jupiter's hugs bring endless cheer!

So if you seek a cosmic friend,
Look to the giant, your joy won't end.
In swirling storms or tranquil beams,
Jupiter's love fuels all our dreams.

Tales from the Cosmic Sea

In the cosmic sea, where starlights play,
I catch a comet on a bright blue day.
With jellyfish planets, we swim and glide,
Stories of wonder, in waves we ride.

Octopi aliens wave hello,
In this weird sea, I'm in the glow.
We trade tall tales with moons so bold,
Of space-time wonders that never get old.

Nautical miles on the Milky Way,
I surf through nebulas, daring and gay.
With rockets for surfboards, we carve and twist,
In this shimmering sea, there's nothing amiss.

So join the fun in this stellar spree,
Where laughter echoes in waves so free.
Under the stars, we're all at play,
In the cosmic sea, let's drift away.

Beyond the Event Horizon

Beyond the horizon, what lies in wait?
A cosmic circus, oh what a fate!
With black holes dancing like party pros,
Gravity isn't all, as everyone knows.

I tripped over time, what a blunder,
Fell through a warp, now I'm filled with wonder.
The space-time clowns juggle with glee,
Making me laugh till I can't see!

Galactic delights and quantum quips,
We sip on starlight, take hearty sips.
With all that laughter, I lose my way,
But in this madness, I choose to stay.

So if you tumble through cosmic fear,
Know beyond that hole, joy's always near.
With a wink and a giggle, we float, we rise,
Beyond the event, we share our skies.

Solaris Dreams

In a rocket made of cheese,
I zoom past the moon with ease.
Stars wink like a mischievous sprite,
As I dance with comets at night.

Galactic giggles fill the air,
Floating in zero-gravity flair.
Jupiter jests with a stormy grin,
Inviting me for a spin!

With Saturn's rings, I play hopscotch,
Counting asteroids—oh what a botch!
Cosmic clowns in a wild parade,
In this universe of fun, we're made.

Waking up in a nebula's glow,
Dreams of Mars with a disco show.
Alien friends all join the feast,
In Solaris dreams, we dance like beasts!

Interstellar Conversations

Two aliens chat over interstellar brew,
One sips coffee, the other a goo.
They laugh as they swap tales of old,
While meteors buzz, daring and bold.

"Did you hear about that wormhole gag?"
One alien snorted, almost to brag.
"He slipped through and ended up in a bar,
Singing karaoke to a moonlit guitar!"

'I've danced with a black hole, you know,'
Said the other with a theatrical show.
'It spun me around, what a wild ride!
I came out dizzy but filled with pride!'

As planets twirl and supernovae gleam,
Their laughter echoes, a cosmic dream.
In this universe arms spread wide,
They're best buddies with stars as guide.

Celestial Haiku

Stars giggle softly,
Planets spin in silly dance,
Comets chase the moon.

Saturn's rings sparkle,
Jovial dust in a whirl,
Galaxies spin bright.

Galactic birds sing,
Orbiting in laughter's tune,
Cosmos' playful smiles.

Falling Into the Black

A trip through the void, what a lark,
  Wheeling, dealing, in the dark.
  Falling into a black hole swirl,
  Holding on tight, give it a twirl.

Lost socks float by, what a sight!
  Intergalactic laundry in flight.
Do they dance or just hang around?
Now that's a cosmic lost and found!

My spaceship hiccups, a humorous tease,
  "Refuel with stardust, if you please."
With giggles and gaffes, we dash ahead,
Sailing through silence with joy, not dread.

So here's to the journeys of cosmic lore,
With riffs and jokes, we always explore.
  In the darkness, let laughter ignite,
  Falling into the black, holding on tight!

The Gravity of Longing

In a rocket made of dreams,
I floated past the cosmic beams.
With stars as my companions bright,
I pondered love beyond the night.

Yet every time I reached for more,
I tripped on asteroids galore.
To chase a heart across the void,
I found myself just rather annoyed.

I waved at Venus, gave a shout,
But she just laughed and spun about.
In love with space, but it feels strange,
The laws of physics, they won't change.

So here I drift, a little lost,
In the universe, I'm paying the cost.
But laughter echoes through the dark,
As I float on, a wobbly spark.

A Sonnet for Celestial Wanderers

Oh voyagers of cosmic fate,
You traverse through the stars that wait.
A twist of fate in every glide,
While dodging meteors, we abide.

Your ships are quirky, sleek, and round,
With rubber bands for engines found.
The universe is quite a prank,
As black holes laugh, the void's debank.

Yet off you go with quirky cheer,
To seek new worlds and conquer fear.
But watch your snacks, they float away,
And end up stuck where comets sway.

So raise a glass of cosmic juice,
To those who brave the endless use.
For in this vast and wacky show,
We sip and laugh as galaxies grow.

Moonlit Reflections on Jupiter's Shores

On Jupiter, we build our dreams,
With giant storms and swirling beams.
We play hopscotch with the moons,
While serenading cosmic tunes.

The tides are wild, the waves are high,
As funky fish swim as they fly.
We ride the winds and laugh so loud,
While Jupiter stands, proud and clouded.

But what's a beach without some sand?
Our grains are made of starry land.
We dance with aliens, break the rules,
In our vibrant, spacey, oceans' schools.

As night falls down in hues of gold,
The laughter echoes, tales retold.
For on these shores, we are all free,
In Jupiter's embrace, just you and me.

The Poetry of Light Years

Oh light years long, where time's a jest,
We measure dreams, yet fail the quest.
With laughter ringing through the span,
We ponder just what time began.

Each twinkle holds a tale to tell,
Of planets soft and comets' swell.
Yet chasing light can feel quite bumpy,
When every turn makes minds a scrumpy.

In cosmic pubs, we toast our fate,
To distances that test our plate.
Our pints are filled with stardust cheer,
As we repeat the same old year.

So raise your glass and make a rhyme,
For in this vastness, we find time.
A funny dance on cosmic sands,
Where light years stretch and laughter stands.

Cosmic Heartbeats

In the cosmos, my heart skips,
Dancing with aliens, doing flips.
Starry-eyed and full of glee,
They laugh at my attempts to flee.

Floating by a comet's tail,
My sense of direction gone pale.
Planets giggle at my plight,
As I try to anchor in the night.

Asteroids toss me like a ball,
Pew-pew sounds, I hear it all.
I wave to Martians, they wave back,
In this wacky, galactic track.

With cosmic jokes and witty puns,
I'm the jester among the suns.
Orbiting laughter, shining bright,
What a joyride in the night!

Stellar Serenades

Singing to the stars above,
With a galactic grin to shove.
Moonbeams join in my refrain,
Together we dance, what a gain!

Jupiter rolls with laughter loud,
While Saturn's rings form a crowd.
A comet joins, oh what a sight,
As we croon away the night.

Planets sway in solar breeze,
I trip over space dust with ease.
Singing songs of a cosmic kind,
While black holes pull and unwind.

With echoes of laughter and joy,
A stellar ballad, oh boy!
Shooting stars fall, a bow we take,
In this grand galactic wake!

Beyond the Nebula's Embrace

Past the stars, I lose my way,
Navigating with a chicken sway.
Funky galaxies twirl around,
In this stellar circus, I'm spellbound.

A nebula hugs me, nice and tight,
Is this love or a space fright?
Meteorites come to join the fun,
Party's on, space has begun!

Aliens serve space snacks galore,
With twinkling drinks, I want more!
While UFOs play hide and seek,
We unzip the galaxies, so unique.

In this vacuum of joy and cheer,
I giggle at all I hold dear.
Beyond the cosmos' warm embrace,
Funny dreams fuel this wild chase!

Echoes of the Infinite

Whispers of stars fill the air,
Tales of mishaps, beyond compare.
The moon rolls its eyes at my clumsiness,
Saying, 'Child, you're a cosmic mess!'

Shooting stars take bets on me,
How many spins 'til I hit a tree?
Cosmic mishaps are what I serve,
When I take a wild curve!

Galaxies giggle in galaxy cafes,
As I trip on light years and space rays.
Planets pass by with a knowing glance,
Throwing confetti, join the dance!

With echoes of laughter all around,
Together we spin, round and round.
In this infinite jest, I see,
Life's a comedy, funny and free!

Driftwood Among the Stars

In cosmic seas, we float along,
With floating logs, we sing our song.
Asteroids bump, like clumsy friends,
In a dance of fate that never ends.

The moon is cheese, we take a slice,
Giggles echo, oh what a nice!
We toast with stars, a fizzy cheer,
As aliens wave from a disco sphere.

Galactic waves, we ride the flow,
With pine cone hats, we steal the show.
Nuts and bolts turn into glee,
In this woodsy space jamboree.

So here's to drifters in the sky,
With wooden hearts that laugh and sigh.
Comets chase, with a "Whoops! Oh dear!"
In the universe, we disappear.

Orbits of Emotion

Round and round, emotions spin,
Like planets dance, we laugh and grin.
Joy's a comet, bright and bold,
While sadness floats, a tale retold.

Gravitational pulls of silly toys,
Turn simple whims into noisy joys.
We giggle hard at wobbly moons,
Hopping through galactic tunes.

Pressure builds like a soda pop,
As we whirl and twirl, we can't just stop.
Asteroids shape our little hearts,
Creating laughter in every part.

So let's orbit, no need for fright,
In this cosmic ballet, pure delight.
With each flip and twist of fate,
We find the humor, oh, so great!

Comets Passing

Zipping by, those comets play,
With silly grins, they save the day.
Whiskered tails like furry friends,
In frolicsome games that never end.

They zoom, they dart, like shooting stars,
Leaving trails of candy bars.
We catch them in a net of dreams,
To share our laughs in moonbeam gleams.

With cosmic hops and giggly spins,
They steal our hearts, like mischievous twins.
Popcorn bursts in the meteor shower,
As we munch, they twinkle and tower.

So watch them dance, those comet pals,
Underneath the laughing gals.
In this universe of gleeful sights,
We cheer them on through starry nights.

Solitary in Stardust

Alone, I drift on stardust plush,
A fuzzy cloud in a cosmic hush.
Yet giggles echo from afar,
As shooting stars play peek-a-boo par.

In solitude, I ride the wave,
Bouncing light with a goofy rave.
A pogo stick on Saturn's ring,
Where cosmic creatures laugh and sing.

I wear my space suit made of fluff,
With rocket boots and earful stuff.
Chasing dreams in a bubble trail,
Through quirky realms where silliness prevails.

So lonely? Not with a twinkling crew,
In this playful cosmos, laughter's true.
Solitary? No, I've got a blast,
In a galaxy where joy is vast.

Ephemeral Celestial Beings

In the cosmos, stars dance a jig,
Wobbling like jelly, each one a big wig.
They twinkle and giggle, a silly delight,
Making wishes on comets that zoom past at night.

Planets wear hats made of dust and of dreams,
Sipping on stardust and cosmic ice creams.
A moon made of cheese, how would it taste?
Let's gather the crumbs, no need to waste!

A shooting star slips, with a wink and a grin,
Hiding its blush, it knows it can't win.
While aliens chuckle in ships made of goo,
They're playing charades, with a game of peek-a-boo.

Galaxies giggle, swirling in play,
They tickle the cosmos, in their own silly way.
With marshmallow moons that bounce off the sun,
They throw cosmic confetti, oh what perfect fun!

Galaxies in Our Eyes

Comets slip past like a sneaky pet cat,
While we gaze at the sky, wearing space-themed hats.
Each twinkle a joke, light-years in length,
Making us laugh, with joyous strength.

Stars play hide-and-seek with their glowing friends,
Shining their chuckles as the day ends.
In twilight's embrace, they settle down tight,
Sharing funny tales till they fade out of sight.

Planets roll over, stuck in a spin,
Grinning at Earth with a cheeky grin.
They spin tales of colors and alien bands,
With music of gravity, nobody understands.

If you look closely, you might just find,
A giddy little neutron, wildly unkind.
Tickled by fusion, bursting with glee,
In the great cosmic circus, come watch and see!

The Pulses of Ionized Gas

In the heart of the nebula, laughter erupts,
With ionized gas making funny abrupts.
Pulsing like bass in a cosmic club,
The stars are a disco, come join the hub!

Clouds of gases swirl in a colorful fray,
Making up stories in a playful way.
Electrons boogie, in rhythm and time,
Pulsing and prancing, to a cosmic rhyme.

Supernovae burst with a pop and a cheer,
Scatter sparkles of joy, oh what a sight here!
The Milky Way giggles, a galactic delight,
As quasars are nodding, saying "What a night!"

With each cosmic bubble, a tickle they give,
For the laughter of gas is how we all live.
In the expanse of the void, where jokers reside,
The universe chuckles, with humor as its guide.

Moonlight Reverberations

The moon casts shadows with a wink and a twist,
Making night critters giggle and tryst.
Whispers of silvery laughter resound,
As moonbeams play tag with the starlit ground.

Crickets hold concerts beneath lunar beams,
Singing of love and outlandish dreams.
While fireflies dance in a playful parade,
In the moon's warm glow, hilarity's made.

The tides keep giggling, shifting with glee,
For moonlight is magic, so wondrous to see.
A tide pool of chuckles, it sparkles and flows,
Leaving everyone wondering how laughter grows.

In the realm of the night, where giggles unite,
Stars share their jokes, making darkness feel bright.
So let's ride the waves of lunar delight,
And join in the joy of this magical night!

Chasing Aurora's Dances

In the sky, lights do swirl,
As fluffy clouds start to twirl.
Aliens laugh, waving their arms,
Chasing colors, spreading charms.

Worms in spacesuits do race,
Strutting proud in this vast place.
They trip over stars, what a sight,
Now they dance in pure delight.

With a giggle, a comet flies,
Tickling moons in the night skies.
Bumping in hues, they all glide,
Shooting rainbows, joy can't hide.

So join the fun, put on your hat,
Dance with aliens, how about that?
Laugh with light, spin with grace,
Chasing auroras in endless space.

Celestial Love Between the Planets

Mars sent Venus a big bouquet,
Roses made of rocks, hip-hip-hooray!
Jupiter pouted, "I'm too big for love,"
While Saturn laughed, gazing from above.

Pluto, lonely on the side,
Wants a partner for a cosmic ride.
He sends a message, "Send me a friend!"
Maybe one day, love will transcend.

Neptune and Uranus share a waltz,
Confetti made of ice, what a pulse!
Moons join in with a twist and twirl,
In this dance, beauty does unfurl.

Each planet joins in, raising a cheer,
In this galaxy of love, most sincere.
Beyond the stars, a cosmic fling,
In this universe, joy takes wing.

Tales from the Cosmic Frontier

Once a star lost its shiny glow,
A cowboy comet rode the flow.
He lassoed clouds made of gas,
With laughter loud, in a heavenly class.

Asteroids raced in wild confusion,
Turning unplanned, in light's delusion.
One bumped a star and got a cry,
"Oops, my bad!" as they both flew by.

A curious black hole swallowed a mirth,
Spitting out jokes, for all it's worth.
It chuckled deep, a laugh so wide,
As space travelers giggled and tried to hide.

With every comet's tail, stories unfold,
In the vastness, adventures bold.
So grab your chair, cast your net,
In cosmic tales, we'll never forget.

Harmony in the Cosmic Silence

In silence, stars do hum and sing,
A melody from the cosmos brings.
Galaxies sway, oh what a sight,
In this vast expanse, day turns to night.

Satellites spin, keeping the beat,
While meteors dance in a rhythmic heat.
With funny faces, they swing around,
In the silence, joy does abound.

A neutron star on a violin,
Plays a tune, oddly thin.
While comets clap with their tails,
Creating harmony on cosmic trails.

So listen close to the sounds of space,
Where humor and music find their place.
In the cosmic silence, laughter rings,
A joyful dance in these celestial swings.

Galactic Reveries

In a rocket made of foil,
Astronauts make a lot of noise.
They snack on Tang and gummies,
Floating by their favorite toys.

Stars above are giggling loud,
As comets race in silly ways.
They play tag with the cosmic dust,
And dance in nebulous ballets.

Aliens look through their glass,
Scoffing at our human quirks.
They laugh at Earth and all its fuss,
And mimic our most awkward perks.

When we land on Mars with glee,
Expect a party from the Martians.
With disco balls and zero-G,
Who knew that space had such precautions?

Celestial Eclipses

Oh, the moon decided to hide,
Behind the Earth in a game of peek.
The sun just rolled its fiery eyes,
"Come on, buddy, what's with the sneak?"

Planets giggle, spinning 'round,
Making faces, what a sight!
Every eclipse is a cosmic joke,
As stars burst out in sheer delight.

Jupiter throws a launch party,
With rings that wobble, that provoke.
Saturn wearing funny hats,
While Venus tries to share a joke.

But when clouds cover the show,
The universe gives a little sigh.
Yet laughter echoes through the void,
As celestial bodies wink and pry.

Alien Whispers in the Void

Little green men in a pickle,
Trying to make sense of TikTok.
They swap their gadgets for our snacks,
And laugh at humans in a flock.

On Mondays they have asteroid brunch,
Where meteorites get the best tea.
They gossip softly 'bout black holes,
And shake their heads in cosmic glee.

Their rockets run on laughter juice,
Which makes them soar like silly kites.
When they land, they jump and shout,
"Take us to your leader; it's a riot!"

They love our quirks, our earthly charms,
And scribble notes in swirling scrolls.
Who knew the vastness held such fun?
Even out there, joy patrolled.

Orbiting Dreams of Stardust

Round and round the planets go,
Spinning tales of cosmic cheer.
Satellites hum their tunes, you know,
While comets wipe away a tear.

Chasing dreams on trails of light,
Space bears whispers, oh so sly.
Asteroids crack jokes in their flight,
As shooting stars flit by with a sigh.

Alien pets chase sunbeams bright,
While space cats dance from star to star.
They tug at gravity with delight,
And giggle at our cars from afar.

Oh, the universe loves a prank,
From black holes to the Milky Way.
In cosmic jest, we've got a tank,
Of laughter, fueling every day.

Dance of the Comet's Tail

A comet zooms with a sparkly show,
Its tail spins round, like a cosmic disco.
Aliens laugh, they twirl and sway,
Inviting the planets to join the fray.

With glittery trails and a wiggly twist,
Even black holes can't resist the twist.
Stars twinkle bright, join the clown parade,
Who knew the cosmos could be such a charade?

Martians giggle, with eyes so wide,
While astronauts munch on moon cheese, side by side.
Comets can dance; that's what I declare,
As meteors tumble without a care.

So grab your friends, let's zoom like the light,
In the galactic dance, all is delight.
With music of planets, let laughter prevail,
For tonight we're part of the comet's tail!

Lost Among the Stars

Floating away, oh where did I go?
Chasing a star with a humorous glow.
Planets are giggling, they think it's a game,
As I try to catch them, it's all the same.

Lost in the cosmos, with aliens bold,
Trading my snacks for some tales to be told.
One offers laughter, another a rhyme,
While I keep bumping into space-time.

A meteor shower, with confetti like rain,
Each burst is a joke; I can't keep my brain.
Floating in glee, I forget my way,
But who needs a map when you're here to play?

So raise a glass of starlight tonight,
To laughter and joy, feel the cosmic light.
I may be lost, yet I'm never alone,
With amusing companions, the universe is home!

Interstellar Lullabies

In the quiet of night, hear the stars sing,
A lullaby woven from cosmic bling.
Whispering wishes on twilight's embrace,
Tickling the void with a warm, gentle grace.

Stars hum sweet tunes that float through the air,
While comets do pirouettes without a care.
Wormholes join in, with a twist and a spin,
A spacey ballet, for the sleepy within.

Planets all snore, in their orbits they dream,
Of ice cream asteroids and marshmallow beams.
Each twinkling flash, a wink in the night,
Reminds silly souls everything's alright.

So close your eyes tight, let the starlight parade,
With chuckles from Venus and jokes from the shade.
Drift off to sleep, as galaxies sway,
In the comfort of laughter, you're safe on your way.

Whispers from a Distant Planet

A planet far away sends a whispering breeze,
With laughs of the creatures that tickle the trees.
They dance in the light of a jolly big moon,
Singing sweet tunes to the shy little dunes.

They poke and they prod, teasing Earthlings around,
Juggling with stardust, they leap off the ground.
Floating in laughter, it's quite the galore,
Each giggle a rocket that's ready to soar.

With pranks on the comets, let's have a grand time,
From globby green figures to planets that rhyme.
So join in the fun, wherever you dwell,
In the wild cosmic giggle, we all find our spell.

For on this far rock, joy knows no bounds,
With every soft whisper, a curiosity surrounds.
So catch a few chuckles, and let your day shine,
In the universe's laughter, we all intertwine!

Collective Constellation

In the sky, they like to play,
Stars dance around, a cosmic ballet.
Twinkling tales of distant friends,
While comets giggle, the laughter never ends.

Galaxies swirl in a humorous sight,
Asteroids bumping, oh what a fright.
Neighbors in orbit, what a wild crew,
Even black holes have jokes, it's true!

Planets with quirks, they spin and twirl,
Saturn wears rings, all shiny with pearl.
Mars grumbles slightly, "I need a snack,"
While Jupiter scoffs, "I've got your back!"

Laughter echoes through cosmic halls,
Echoing softly, as the universe calls.
Together we jest in endless delight,
As we float through this wonderful night.

Twilight Among the Planets

In twilight glow, planets unite,
Sharing secrets in the soft starlight.
Venus whispers, "I'm feeling bold,"
While Neptune chuckles, "I'm icy and cold!"

Mercury zips with a speed-induced grin,
"Catch me if you can," with a cheeky spin.
Earth pretends to be calm and wise,
While the moon pulls pranks under dark skies.

Quiet Saturn, rings in a swirl,
Laughs at the chaos of each little world.
"Come join my party, it's ready to start!"
As they all dance with a cosmic heart.

Together they giggle, a celestial show,
Orbiting laughter wrapped in a glow.
In the twilight among the bright,
They're friends forever in the starry night.

A Love Letter to the Universe

Dear Universe, you're vast and wide,
Your stars hold secrets that brightly glide.
Your black holes tug at my heartstrings,
While pulsars remind us of funny things.

I adore your planets, each with flair,
Jupiter's storms and Venus's glare.
You've wrapped me in wonder, it's plain to see,
Even supernovae share their love with me.

Oh, comets with tails that sparkle and spin,
Whispering tales, as if they're my kin.
Your galaxies twirl in a joyous dance,
As I ponder my life and cosmic romance.

So here's my letter, written in jest,
To my favorite universe, you are the best.
With laughter and joy, I send my cheer,
To the laughter-filled skies, I hold so dear.

Flight Through Saturn's Rings

Zooming through rings, it's quite a ride,
Waving at Saturn, my interstellar guide.
Dust and ice, they swirl and play,
While I giggle, "Just another day!"

A spaceship ballet in the cosmic breeze,
Dodging playful rocks with expert ease.
"Hey, watch out!" I shout with glee,
As a ringlet twirls and dances around me.

Racing past moons, who wink and flirt,
Floating in zero-g, oh isn't it a perk?
With Saturn's smile shining bright,
It's a whimsical journey into the night.

Surrounded by laughter, as stars collide,
In this flight through the rings, my joy can't hide.
And as I zip through this dazzling scene,
I'm living a dream, oh what a keen machine!

Voices from the Galactic Seas

In the stars, the fish do swim,
They wear tiny hats, so very prim.
They sing songs about cosmic cheese,
And dance with glee on solar breeze.

Jellyfish float with a twinkling glow,
Chatting with planets, putting on a show.
A whale sings deep, a tune quite neat,
With asteroids clapping to the beat.

Octopus pilots in ships of light,
With tentacles waving, oh what a sight!
They dive through comets, sipping tea,
Giggling at stardust, wild and free.

So if you gaze up at night's dark dome,
Know that up there, it's a cosmic home.
With laughter and joy, they dance in peace,
Voices from seas where wonders never cease.

The Moon's Secret Winks

Oh little moon, with your glowing face,
You wink at me from your shining place.
With craters like smiles and beams so bright,
You whisper jokes in the dead of night.

You tell of dreams that astronauts chase,
Of dancing stars in a merry race.
With a giggle, you hide behind your veil,
While shooting stars sing a silly tale.

There's cheese on your surface, or so they say,
But I've seen it melt on a sunny day.
You chuckle softly as comets pass,
Your laughter ripples like shimmering glass.

So join me, dear moon, in this cosmic jest,
Your whims and wonders, they are the best.
With every wink, a delightful cheer,
In the lunar light, we'll laugh without fear.

Stardust Memories

In a galaxy where the laughter flows,
Stardust memories dance in rows.
They twirl and swirl, a shimmering sight,
Playing hide and seek in the cosmic night.

Comets slide in a playful chase,
Painting the void with color and grace.
Each sprinkle of gold, a story to tell,
Of giggling planets that know how to gel.

Nebulas wear hats that swirl and spin,
With playful antics, they draw me in.
They whisper secrets of funny delight,
Under the watchful gaze of starlit night.

So gather your thoughts from the cosmic spree,
In this universe, so wild and free.
With stardust memories and laughter bright,
We'll weave our tales in the endless light.

Echoes of the Universe

In the vastness where echoes collide,
The giggles of galaxies swell with pride.
They bounce off stars in a joyful tune,
As comets swing by like a dancing balloon.

Black holes chuckle, deep and profound,
As planets and asteroids whirl all around.
They call out names in a rhyming spree,
The universe giggles with cosmic glee.

Supernovas burst into fits of laughter,
Creating new stars as happily after.
With whispers of joy from star to star,
Echoing fun from near and far.

So listen closely, and you may find,
The echoes of humor, sweet and kind.
In the universe wide, where jokes do prevail,
Laughter and love are the ultimate tale.

Voyage Through Dark Matter

In a ship made of cheese, we sail so free,
Zipping past stars and a dancing bee.
Gravity's gone, we're floaty and light,
Chasing a comet that looks like a kite.

Singing with aliens, their voices are odd,
They dance like they're plugged into some cosmic rod.
With lasers for arms and googly eyes,
They pop out their heads and surprise us with pies.

Planets we pass, they're all spinning fast,
Waving to moons, we've made friendships last.
An echo of laughter, our folly is grand,
Who knew outer space was so ticklish and planned?

With every new orbit, a giggle we share,
Even black holes seem to have flair.
So here's to the journey, with humor intact,
In this cosmic dance, we're never off-track.

Echoes of Distant Galaxies

Twirling through nebulae, what a wild spree,
Whispers of stars calling, "Come dance with me!"
Galaxies giggle as they whirl around,
We join in the ruckus, our laughter profound.

Asteroids chuckle, with silly little spins,
Who knew space rocks could have so many grins?
They roll like they're playing a cosmic game,
Shouting, "Hey Earthlings, we're not all the same!"

We skip on the rings of a giant old friend,
Sipping space juice that seems to transcend.
With bubbles and burbles that tickle the throat,
We toast to the wonders of this cosmic boat.

As echoes of laughter ripple back in time,
Every star shows its funny side in rhyme.
So let's keep exploring, in humor unite,
A galaxy's heart filled with pure delight.

Asteroid Through Time

Riding a rock through a comical past,
Each era tickles us, racing so fast.
Dinosaurs dance, in their silly old ways,
While cavemen prepare for an astrological craze.

From future to present, what's next on the queue?
Flying past robots who haven't a clue.
With gadgets that blink, and lights that will flash,
They trip over circuits and end with a crash.

We giggle through ages, from caverns to space,
Finding lost items, like socks out of place.
Each time loop is warped, a fresh funny stream,
History's moments, the quirkiest dream.

With a wink and a nod, we barrel on through,
Past timelines and giggles, in a cosmic brew.
So here's to our trip through the fabric of time,
We'll keep laughing and dancing, all in our prime.

Stratospheric Soliloquy

Floating up high in a whimsical mood,
Tickling the clouds, feeling light and good.
A bird passing by gives a curious glance,
Wondering if we're just a part of its dance.

The sun winks down, wearing shades oh so cool,
While stars play hopscotch, like kids after school.
We wave at the moon, who's polishing cheese,
Shouting, "Save a slice for us, if you please!"

With laughter that echoes miles high in the sky,
We giggle at planets that spin and sigh.
In the stratosphere's bubble, our joy knows no bounds,
Chasing soft comets that laugh with their sounds.

So here's to the journey where whimsy is queen,
In this colorful world, we'll always be seen.
Floating forever, like bubbles in wine,
In this bunch of giggles, we endlessly shine.

Astral Serenade

Floating in my fancy chair,
I waved to stars without a care.
My coffee drifted far away,
And splashed a comet in dismay.

My cat's a pro at zero g,
She pounced on meteors with glee.
Her fur, like stardust, starts to flow,
As we play tag with the moonbeams' glow.

We danced with aliens in the night,
Wobbling 'round in sheer delight.
They taught me how to make a sound,
That echoes in the vacuum found.

The universe chuckled loud and bright,
As I forgot to turn off the light.
My ship's ablaze with agitated sparks,
But laughter's my fuel; it fills the dark.

Dreaming in Zero Gravity

I tripped on air while dreaming wide,
Bouncing off a cosmic slide.
Asteroids winked, oh what a tease,
As I spun 'round like a swirling breeze.

In this realm of float and sway,
My socks decided to drift away.
They found a black hole, made a friend,
A sock puppet party that won't end.

Planets giggle, stars take bets,
On how fast I can lose my pets.
But here in space, it's all in fun,
Chasing laughter, we always run.

I'll write a ballad to the sun,
About my socks and their great run.
In zero g, there's no goodbye,
Just a comical wink from the sky.

Galactic Reverie

In a spaceship shaped like a shoe,
I take my dog for a stroll too.
He sniffs at stars with keen delight,
Chasing aliens into the night.

We sing along with Martian bands,
Playing tunes with rubber hands.
With every note, we swirl and spin,
As Saturn grins and lets us in.

A comet whizzes, like a joke,
Throwing sparks against the smoke.
My dog just barks at Saturn's rings,
"Fetch the rover!" he joyfully sings.

Galactic dreams, oh what a sight,
My pup and I chase endless light.
In this cosmic playground so free,
We laugh at gravity's decree.

Echoes of the Void

Heard a giggle in the void,
A cosmic prank, I'm overjoyed.
Space cows jumped over the moon,
Mooing melodies, a joyful tune.

I floated by a taco stand,
With cosmic salsa — how grand!
When I bit, it launched me high,
Spinning with a laugh, oh my!

Asteroids danced like disco lights,
With funky moves, oh what a sight!
Gravity forgot its heavy tune,
As we boogied by a flying spoon.

Echoes of laughter filled the air,
Twinkling winks without a care.
In this void so wild and strange,
Every quirk's just a cosmic change.

Starlit Ballad

Up in the sky, the rockets tease,
Floating past planets with silly ease.
A cow jumps by on a cosmic dream,
While Martians choke on their whipped cream.

Laughter echoes, a galactic joke,
While astronauts dance, and satellites poke.
In zero gravity, they giggle and spin,
A quirky tale where chaos begins.

Stars wink playfully as they collide,
In this universe, there's nowhere to hide.
With comets wearing hats that are bright,
The cosmic circus is pure delight.

So let's toast to the stars, raise a glass,
For every misstep, in this stellar class.
In the realm of space, where humor is key,
We'll drift through the cosmos, wild and free.

Orbiting Memories

Galactic geese in a rocket parade,
Waddling around, not a worry displayed.
They honk at the stars, making quite the scene,
With spacesuits on, looking so serene.

A comet named Fred loves to sing out loud,
While asteroids clap, gathering a crowd.
They share ancient tales with a giggle or two,
In the wonder of what interstellar friends do.

The moon plays chess with a satellite friend,
Creating new rules that will never end.
While nebula clouds crack a cosmic pun,
Laughing at planets that skip and run.

In orbits of laughter, we twirl and glide,
With memories spinning in a joyous ride.
Let's dance among stars, in this silly embrace,
With a wink from the cosmos, we find our place.

Where the Stars Will Sing

On a shooting star, a cat takes a ride,
With dreams of space fish swimming by side.
They strum on guitars made of moonbeams,
While cosmic rays tickle, igniting their dreams.

The Milky Way's choir starts belting out tunes,
One note for the planets, another for moons.
A raucous affair, where laughter is rich,
In the cosmic cabaret, they switch and twitch.

Stars in top hats offer comics to read,
With cosmic carrots as their favorite feed.
They juggle stardust and wiggle their toes,
In this stellar cabaret, anything goes.

So gather 'round, friends, let's sing through the night,
With twinkling laughter and sheer delight.
In the realms above, where joy takes its fling,
Together we'll dance where the stars will sing.

Nebula Lullabies

In a nebula night where dreams take flight,
Clouds of candy floss drift softly in sight.
With space whales humming their soothing refrain,
They rock us to sleep on a cosmic train.

The stars are the lanterns that guide our way,
As rocket raccoons come out to play.
They whisper sweet tales of where they have been,
Twirling through planets, in laughter they spin.

Galaxies cuddle, sharing secrets with glee,
In this quiet moment, just you and me.
We'll float on our dreams like balloons in the dark,
While the universe hums with a gentle spark.

So close your eyes tight, let the night take its hold,
With nebula lullabies, warm and bold.
A journey through giggles beneath cosmic skies,
Where mischief and wonder in harmony lies.

Planetary Dreams

In a realm of floating cheese,
I danced with moonlit bees.
Jupiter laughed, swelling bright,
While Saturn spun in sheer delight.

Comets wore their rainbow hats,
Nearby, a giggling group of cats.
Twinkling stars cheered with glee,
In this world of whimsy and spree.

Aliens served cosmic pies,
Made of stardust and moonlit skies.
With each bite, we soared up high,
On marshmallow clouds, oh my!

So here we dream, with joy we beam,
In this universe, wild as a dream.
A place where laughter fills the air,
In planetary dreams, beyond compare.

Lost in the Milky Way

I took a trip on a flying pie,
Through caramel clouds, oh so spry.
Doughnut ships sailed smooth and bright,
As I laughed at stars in the night.

Martians played cards, quite a sight,
While asteroids danced, thrilling and light.
I lost my wallet near a black hole,
But found a sock with a quirky goal.

Galactic gophers ran a race,
Chasing comets with silly grace.
I cheered them on, while sipping juice,
In my space pants, feeling loose.

Lost in wonder, I twirled and spun,
In the Milky Way, having fun.
With interstellar giggles all around,
In cosmic chaos, joy is found.

The Celestial Canvas

Stars paint smiles on the night,
With every brushstroke, pure delight.
Planets waltz in hues so bright,
Crafting a scene of joy and flight.

Nebulas giggle, oh so spry,
While comets zoom, kissing the sky.
In this gallery, laughter reigns,
A masterpiece free from chains.

Each meteor shower a brilliant spark,
Lighting up night, like joy in the dark.
I twirl with joy on this sky-high stage,
An artist's whimsy, in cosmic rage.

The stars and I, bound in this game,
In the celestial canvas, all the same.
With colors of laughter, we intertwine,
In a universe silly, yet so divine.

Midnight's Cosmic Dance

Beneath a disco ball of moons,
We waltz with aliens to funky tunes.
Shooting stars join in the chance,
As we all groove in a cosmic dance.

Gravity takes a cheeky break,
While comets twist and the planets shake.
We float like bubbles, giggles galore,
In this midnight jam, we crave more!

Aliens twirl with robotic flair,
And space hamsters conquer the air.
With laughter echoing through the night,
The universe sparkles, oh what a sight!

So join the fun, don't miss this chance,
For joy awaits in midnight's dance.
In the glimmer of stars, laughter spins,
As cosmic chaos eternally begins.

Synchronizing with the Celestial

In a rocket made of cheese,
With a cat who plays the flute.
We danced among the planets,
To a tune that's quite astute.

The moon wore polka dots,
And Jupiter had a hat.
We laughed until we floated,
While the stars chimed, "What of that?"

With gravity on vacation,
We spun like tops in bliss.
In this cosmic celebration,
We found a world in a twist.

So if you hear a giggle,
From the void, don't be alarmed.
It's just a cosmic riddle,
In which the universe charmed.

Quantum Heartstrings

Atoms jiggle with delight,
As we squeeze them into tunes.
They dance with light and laughter,
Under quantum disco moons.

String theory plays a chord,
That echoes through the void.
We twiddle with our gadgets,
And our logic is destroyed.

Entangled in our giggles,
With particles that play.
We'd swear they're just like toddlers,
Dancing in their own ballet.

So grab a space balloon,
And let the laughter soar.
The universe is fuzzy,
In this quantum-hearted floor.

Celestial Graffiti

Stars scribble on the night,
With crayons made of light.
They leave their doodles scattered,
In a vibrant cosmic flight.

Aliens paint with giggles,
As they spatter colors bright.
We watch with wide-eyed wonder,
At their celestial insight.

Planets with expressive faces,
Cheerfully rotate round.
While comets play the tambourine,
In a joyous cosmic sound.

So if you catch a star smile,
Or hear a meteor's cheer.
Know that the universe doodles,
In a language we hold dear.

A Symphony of Stars

In a concert under skies,
The stars are in their rows.
With violins made of stardust,
They play as each one glows.

Planets clap their tiny hands,
While comets whistle tunes.
A black hole sways in rhythm,
To the music of the moons.

Galaxies form the orchestra,
With twinkling lights that spark.
Each note travels through the cosmos,
Like a playful little lark.

So join the cosmic concert,
Tap your toes in time.
With the universe as our stage,
We laugh in perfect rhyme.

Infinite Orbital Pathways

In a ship made of cheese, we drift and we spin,
Chasing bright comets, with wide grins we grin.
A galaxy of giggles, all floating about,
Navigating planets, there's laughter, no doubt.

Asteroids dance like they're at a grand ball,
While aliens chuckle, we join in the thrall.
With rocket fuel soda, we toast to the stars,
In our cosmic carnival, we're all superstars.

Gravity's just a myth, or so we declare,
We float past the sun in our underwear.
Taking selfies with Martians, it's quite the delight,
Our lunar love story beams brightly at night.

As we twirl through the cosmos, we're never alone,
Bouncing off planets, we make them our home.
With laughter and joy, we'll dance 'til we're old,
On this infinite path, our adventures unfold.

Stardust Memoirs

Once we sat on Saturn, sipping Martian juice,
Laughed at the rings, we felt quite profuse.
Jupiter's storms, they raged with a grin,
Creating a ruckus, they dared us to spin.

In a starship of puns, we floated with glee,
A waltz with a nebula, just you and me.
With each twinkle we laughed, a cosmic delight,
Writing memoirs in stardust, oh what a sight!

Comets with glitter, they zipped by our toes,
Wacky and wild, like a carnival show.
We played peekaboo with a black hole's dark kiss,
In a theft of the moment, nothing's amiss.

Our tales of the galaxy are filled with good cheer,
Whispers of laughter, a universe near.
Among cosmic wonders, we found our bright worth,
In this laughter-filled dance, we embrace the universe.

The Soul of a Distant Star

Oh distant star, with your twinkling glare,
You wink at us softly, like you are aware.
Your jokes are light-years, your rhythm divine,
In the silence of cosmos, your humor does shine.

We chuckle at quasars, all blazing with pride,
Your jokes circle round in the vastness, they glide.
With laughter in orbit, we thrum and we sway,
As you beckon us closer, come join in the play.

Whispers of supernovas echo in space,
As we roll on the rings of your radiant face.
You teach us to dance with the dust in your trail,
In a world of bright chaos, we laugh and we sail.

Your soul holds the secrets, the fun never ends,
In this comedy show, we're the stars' best friends.
So let's toast to the cosmos, our joy like a star,
In the cradle of laughter, we'll wander afar.

Strange Attractors

In the gravity game, we're quirky and bold,
Twisting around in a dance we're told.
With magnets of mirth, we spin through the air,
Our happy little orbits are beyond compare.

In this swirling confetti of cosmic delight,
We giggle with planets that twinkle so bright.
Playing tag with the moons, they come out to play,
In the whirl of the cosmos, we laugh all the way.

Like squirrels in a nebula, we frolic and glide,
Caught in this chaos, stars shining wide.
With peculiar forces, we bounce and we zig,
In the universe's laughter, we dance like a jig.

Strange attractors pull us, keep us in cheer,
Gravity's just a pun, let's make this clear.
With each cosmic breath, joy swirls in a wave,
In this wacky adventure, we're all really brave.

Timeless Journeys through the Cosmos

In a rocket made of tinfoil,
We zoom past stars with great toil.
Astronauts snack on cosmic cheese,
While dodging flying space bees.

Planets dance in a goofy way,
With asteroids that like to play.
Galaxies giggle in the night,
As aliens join in delight.

Jupiter wears a silly hat,
Venus sways like a chubby cat.
Every comet brings a cheer,
Handing out some cosmic beer.

Amongst the moons, we laugh and spin,
Chasing laughter for the win.
Time floats by in a merry race,
In our timeless, wacky space.

Celestial Rhapsody

Singing stars in bright attire,
With meteor showers of wild fire.
Jupiter juggles its moons with flair,
While Saturn's rings dance through the air.

Comets wink as they fly by,
With cheeky grins that make us sigh.
Galaxy spins in a swirling spree,
Sipping stardust tea with glee.

Asteroids play in a rock band,
While cosmic dust fills up the sand.
Nebulas puff like cotton candy,
In a universe that feels so dandy.

Shooting stars give us a show,
With wishes stuck on a cosmic glow.
As laughter echoes through the void,
In this rhapsody we enjoyed.

Celestial Whispers

Whispers float on starlit beams,
Telling tales of our wild dreams.
Galactic gossip fills the air,
As planets spin without a care.

Silly aliens have a chat,
Discussing life with a friendly cat.
Supernovae throw a rave,
While black holes play hide and wave.

Laughter rings in the cosmic night,
As comets zoom for a lunar flight.
Astro-bunnies hop 'round in glee,
In this space of whimsy and esprit.

Stardust tickles the senses right,
In a universe that's full of light.
With every twinkle, a joke is spun,
In celestial whispers, we have fun.

Beyond the Cosmic Veil

Beyond the veil where stars collide,
Funky creatures love to hide.
Dancing comets in glittery gowns,
Joking with the spacey clowns.

Each planet spins with a silly tune,
Joking 'bout their cosmic balloon.
Lightning strikes in a funny way,
As stars play games in bright ballet.

In the depths of a black hole's wink,
We share our jokes and let thoughts sink.
Through cosmic corridors, laughter spreads,
As the universe fills our heads.

So sail with me on this whimsical ride,
Where cosmic humor is our guide.
Together we'll float in joy so vast,
In this journey through stars, we'll ever last.

Whispers in the Dark Matter

In the void where no one peeks,
A rogue comet plays hide and seeks.
Aliens giggle, they can't get far,
On their day off, they sip from a jar.

Stars twinkle like they know a joke,
While asteroids dance, they start to poke.
Cosmic giggles echo through the night,
Astounding each traveler in flight.

Galaxies twist in a silly sprawl,
Celestial creatures have a ball.
A black hole swallows a sad little tune,
Leaving behind a vacuum to swoon.

In dark matter, impersonations thrive,
With starry clowns that bounce and jive.
The Milky Way chuckles, it's a grand affair,
As stardust flutters through the air.

The Nebula's Caress

In a cloud of colors, fuzzy and bright,
Planets wear shades, what a sight!
Comets wear hats made of light,
While galaxies spin with delight.

The nebula giggles, a pink fluffy queen,
Sways to rhythms that can't be seen.
Shooting stars wish for ice cream cones,
As satellites chat in joyful tones.

Asteroids roll like marbles at play,
On a cosmic playground, night and day.
Cosmic rays tickle, oh what a tease,
While the sun just chuckles, as warm as a breeze.

In this colorful haze, laughter stays,
Though in some corners, it secretly plays.
In the vastness above, joy's on display,
Under the stars, come laugh and sway.

Atlas of the Heavens

With star maps tangled in space and time,
The moon hums along to a silly rhyme.
Planets twirl, giving cosmic winks,
Galactic cheese causes asteroids to stink.

Small meteors tumble, they trip and they fall,
Dust particles playing a game of catch-ball.
The universe chuckles, it won't let go,
As stardust giggles in a colorful show.

Saturn's rings jingle like bells in a choir,
Uranus grins, raised eyebrows inquire.
Comets race, they slide on their tails,
While black holes whisper their secret tales.

With laughter in the fabric of night,
Stars clink like glasses in joyous flight.
An atlas of wonders, with maps to explore,
Join in the mirth, there's always more!

Starbound Melodies

Singing planets share a fun little tune,
   Jupiter winks at its jovial moon.
Shooting stars giggle, make wishes fly,
   Meteors dance with a wink and a sigh.

The Sun, a bard, strums with flare,
   Lyrics spill forth, filling the air.
Dance, little comets, across the night sky,
   Chase dream-dust with sparks flying high.

In the frolic of stars and their sparkly cheer,
   Gravity's pull suddenly feels less near.
Celestial bodies swing, twirl in delight,
   While cosmic ballet takes soft flight.

Every note gleams from the heavens above,
   A harmony crafted with laughter and love.
Starbound melodies echo through space,
   Bringing joy to each traveler's face.

www.ingramcontent.com/pod-product-compliance
Lightning Source LLC
Chambersburg PA
CBHW072146200426
43209CB00051B/723